© Cathy McGough 2011

Originally published on May, 2019, in a novel by Cathy McGough as Jump Like a Caribou.
version published in July 2023.
Hardcover NEW version published in June, 2025.

All Rights Reserved. No part of this publication may be reproduced or transmitted in any form or by any means, electronic or mechanical, including photocopy, recording or any other information storage and retrieval system, without prior permission in writing from the publisher at Stratford Living Publishing

ISBN 978-1-990332-34-0
ISBN Print: 978-1-988201-84-9 (Updated 2021)
ISBN HARDCOVER: 978-1-998304-51-6

Cathy McGough has asserted her right under the Copyright, Designs and Patents Act, 1988 to be identified as the author of this work.

Art powered by Canva Pro.

This is a work of fiction. The characters in it are all fiction. Resemblance to any persons living or dead is purely coincidental. Names, characters, places and incidents either are the products of the author's imagination or are used fictitiously.

Dedicated to Shannon.

WHEN YOU'D RATHER STAY IN BED...

HERE'S WHAT YOU CAN DO!

JUMP JUMP JUMP!

LIKE A CARIBOU!

ALWAYS TOO MUCH HOMEWORK TO DO!

HERE'S WHAT YOU CAN DO!

THEN YOU'LL FEEL HAPPY!

THEN YOU'LL BE GLAD!

YOU'LL HAVE THE VERY BEST TIME!

YOU'VE EVER HAD!

ALL YOU'VE GOT TO DO IS...

YOU KNOW WHAT TO DO!

THAT'S BECAUSE THEY KNOW...

EXACTLY WHAT TO DO!

THEN YOU'LL FEEL HAPPY!

THEN YOU'LL BE GLAD!

YOU'LL HAVE THE VERY BEST TIME

YOU'VE EVER HAD!

AND ALL YOU'VE GOT TO DO!

IS...

JUMP JUMP JUMP!

LIKE A CARIBOU!

Jump Series in Paperback:

Jump Like a Caribou!
Jump Like a Kangaroo!
Jump at the Zoo!
Jump and Say P.U.!
Jump and Say Boo!
Jump and Say Valentine's Day Is
For Kids Too!
Jump and Look For a Clue!
Jump and Say Happy Birthday to You!
Jump For Everything Blue!
Jump, Hop and Say Happy Easter To You!
Jump and Say Cock-A-Doodle-Do!
Jump and Sing Da-Do-Do-Do!
Jump and Ask Who? Who?
Jump and Squawk Like a Cockatoo!
Jump and Ask Is It You or Ewe?
Jump and Say There's an Ewww in My Stew!
Jump and Say Merry Christmas To You!
Jump and Cheer Happy New Year!
Jump and Say There's a Moo-Moo in a Tutu!
Jump and Say There's a Hare in My Hair!
Jump and Say My Aunt Ate An Ant!
Jump and Say There's An Aardvark
In The Amusement Park!
Jump and Roar For The Dinosaurs!
Jump and Buzz Like A Bee!
Jump and Flutter Like A Butterfly!
Jump and Pop Like Popcorn!

Jump and Ribbit Like A Frog!
Jump and Snore Like A Koala!
Jump and Snuffle Like A Platypus!
Jump and Grunt Like A Groundhog!
Jump and Say Hello!
Jump and Say Friend!
Jump and Say Peace!
Jump and Say Sky!
Jump and Say Merry Christmas!
Jump and Say Happy New Year!
Jump and Say Fun!
Jump and Say Family!

Clap For Series
Clap for 1!
Clap for 2!
Clap for 3!
Clap for 4!
Clap for 5!
Clap for 6!
Clap for 7!
Clap for 8!
Clap for 9!
Clap for 10!

The Cat Who Said Hello
The Three Boulders
Billy Shakespeare
Billie Shakespeare
Learn To Draw With Symmetry
ABC More Learn to Draw With Symmetry

Non-Fiction
103 Fundraising Ideas For Parent Volunteers With Schools and Teams

www.ingramcontent.com/pod-product-compliance
Lightning Source LLC
Chambersburg PA
CBHW050733010526
44107CB00010B/834